MOVING FO
IN PRAYER

A simple form of daily prayer
for use alone or in groups

compiled by
PETER NOTT
Bishop of Norwich

Illustrated by
Irene Ogden

The Canterbury Press
Norwich

First published 1991 by The Canterbury Press Norwich
(a publishing imprint of Hymns Ancient & Modern Limited
a Registered Charity)
St Mary's Works, St Mary's Plain,
Norwich, Norfolk, NR3 3BH

A catalogue record for this book is available
from the British Library

ISBN 1–85311–048–5

*Typeset and printed in Great Britain by
St Edmundsbury Press Limited
Bury St Edmunds, Suffolk*

Foreword
by the Archbishop of Canterbury

One of the Church of England's greatest assets in its mission to the nation is its parish churches. Sometimes congregations feel burdened by the cost of their upkeep, especially in rural areas, but to retain a recognizable centre of Christian worship and service in every parish is vital to our task in the Decade of Evangelism.

That's why I worry when I come across churches which are under-used for their primary purpose – the worship of God. There are two main reasons for this, especially in the countryside. The first is the reduction in clergy working in rural areas. There is a physical limit to how many Sunday services a clergyman can conduct. And, by a strange irony, our increasing (and entirely correct) appreciation of the Eucharist as the primary act of worship for Christian people has not helped. We have, though, to explore afresh the possibilities of non-eucharistic worship.

In an address to Church of England Readers in Birmingham, I reflected on these matters, and commended the Bishop of Norwich for suggesting that in every community there should be public worship every Sunday at the same time. To bring such a vision about, not only Readers, but the laity more generally, would need to be mobilized.

The Bishop of Norwich's vision is a practical one. And this book shows the essential simplicity of it. Effective corporate prayer does not depend upon the clergy. Nor need the conduct of worship be complicated. I am sure that many others will share my own gratitude to the Bishop of Norwich for following up his own ideas in such a helpful way.

+ George Cantuar

Contents

FOREWORD   *page* 3

INTRODUCTION   5

EXPLANATION: How to use this form of prayer   7

DAILY PRAYER   11

INTERCESSIONS   16

CALENDAR OF PSALMS   23

CALENDAR OF BIBLE READINGS   25

APPENDIX: 'A New Pattern for Sunday Worship'   29

Introduction

It is good for local communities to join together for worship from time to time. It is also right that each community – as each individual Christian – should regularly express their relationship to God in prayer. But in many communities there is no longer a resident parson, so the corporate prayer of the church has often been reduced to match the capacity of available clergy to conduct services. This is particularly the case in rural areas.

How then are we to achieve a pattern of regular corporate prayer in our parishes? It cannot be the responsibility of the clergy alone, nor even of lay readers, who are already often fully-stretched: it is a task for the laity as a whole.

With this in mind, a little while ago I proposed a possible solution (see Appendix), expressing the hope that, even if formal services led by clergy or readers were not possible every week in every church, groups of lay people might pray each week, so maintaining the worship of the church in every community.

This booklet, therefore, has a twofold purpose. First, to provide a simple form of prayer which can be led by anyone. It can be used on Sundays or on weekdays – in church, in a home or, for example, at the beginning or end of meetings. It is basically a simplified version of the services of Morning and Evening Prayer in the ASB.

Secondly, although it is designed to be used by a small group of people, it is also suitable for use alone, as a framework for our personal prayer. The advantage of using a form of common prayer is that, even when we pray alone, we are strengthened and encouraged by being part of an invisible fellowship of those who share the same commitment.

If we are to move forward in evangelism, in love for our neighbour, and in care for God's world, we should begin by moving forward in prayer. It is my hope that *Moving Forward in Prayer* may help us with those first steps.

October 1991   + PETER NORVIC

Explanation
How to use this form of Prayer

The structure is very traditional, consisting of Psalms, Bible readings and Prayers. These are the three elements that one finds in all the ancient forms of Christian daily prayer, which were themselves based on Jewish forms of prayer, which had the same threefold pattern.

The Psalms
The psalms have always been a great source of devotion for the Christian church, and their value is not less today. Following the pattern of the 1928 Prayer Book and ASB, certain verses from a few psalms have been omitted as unsuitable.

The psalms are of course included in the Old Testament, and any version of the Bible can be used for this section. But the best translations of the psalms, which have been composed with a rhythm for speaking aloud or singing, are those contained in the Book of Common Prayer and The Alternative Service Book 1980. The language of the Prayer Book psalms is beautiful and rightly loved, and is the version most familiar to those of an older generation. But the ASB psalms have their merits too (not least because the translation is more accurate), and after years of daily use, many have come to love this version of the psalms as much as the older one.

The Bible Readings
The calendar of Bible readings is designed for use on weekdays. When this form of prayer is used on a Sunday, one of the readings for the Holy Communion on that day would be most suitable.

The calendar provides four months of readings from the Old Testament every year in a two year cycle. Each year there are four months of readings from the Gospels, and four months from the rest of the New Testament. The passages from the Gospels form a very rough chronology of the life of Jesus compiled from the so-called 'synoptic' Gospels – Matthew, Mark and Luke – all of which have a certain amount of material in common. Thus when an incident such as the feeding of the five thousand is recorded by all three writers, only one version is chosen. Most of St John's Gospel is treated separately, because it is so different from the other three.

This is a suggested scheme of Bible reading, which over a two year period will give a familiarity with all the main themes of the Old and New Testaments. But of course there are other schemes of readings which may be used, and variations made in the suggested pattern – for example some people may wish, on Saturdays, to use one of the readings set for the following Sunday's Holy Communion.

The Intercessions
Four intercessions are provided, together with a litany of penitence and a meditation on the Holy Communion to provide one section for use on each week day.

The intercessions should be understood as part of the prayer of the whole church, so they are written in general rather than specific terms. However, it is often desirable to use them more intensively, allowing space for the silent or vocal expression of particular concerns. When used by groups, each section of the intercession may be ended with a versicle and response, such as: 'Lord, in your mercy – Hear our prayer'.

The intercessions provided are a framework within which one can always add one's own intercessions or indeed substitute them for the printed versions.

The Collect for the Day
This is the prayer which is said at the Holy Communion on the previous Sunday. This link helps us to see our daily prayer as a kind of satellite to Sunday, where all our prayer, both private and corporate, finds its focus. The collect on Saturday should be that for the Sunday following.

The Silences
The periods of silence after the reading and the offering of the day are obviously meant to relate to what has immediately preceded them, but they can be used for any purpose. The object is to pause, to reflect, to be still in order to open ourselves to God, and to be alert to his voice, which is most often the 'still small voice' which speaks without words to the depths of our being when we are perfectly still in body and mind.

Daily Prayer

Leader: O Lord, open our lips;
Response: and our mouth shall proclaim your praise.

Leader: Let us worship the Lord.
Response: All praise to his name.

PSALM

(See Calendar on page 23)

At the end of the psalm:

Leader: Glory to the Father, and to the Son,
          and to the Holy Spirit:
Response: as it was in the beginning, is now,
          and shall be for ever. Amen.

BIBLE READING

(See Calendar on page 25)

SILENT MEDITATION

Leader: Lord, fill us with your love in the morning,
    (*or* noonday, *or* evening)
Response: That our days may be spent in joy and in praise.

INTERCESSION

(See pages 16–21)

COLLECT FOR THE DAY

PRAYERS

Leader: Let us offer to God this day:
    the work we do,
    the people we meet,
    the pleasures and the pains;
    that in everything
    we may know the love of Christ,
    and be thankful.

(A short silence follows)

THE LORD'S PRAYER

Together:

(Traditional)

Our Father, who art in heaven, hallowed be thy name;
thy kingdom come;
thy will be done; on earth as it is in heaven.
Give us this day our daily bread.
And forgive us our trespasses,
as we forgive those who trespass against us.
And lead us not into temptation;
but deliver us from evil.
For thine is the kingdom, the power, and the glory,
for ever and ever. Amen.

(Modern)

Our Father in heaven, hallowed be your name,
your kingdom come,
your will be done, on earth as in heaven.
Give us today our daily bread.
Forgive us our sins
as we forgive those who sin against us.
Lead us not into temptation
but deliver us from evil.
For the kingdom, the power, and the glory are yours
now and for ever. Amen.

CLOSING PRAYERS

Leader: Keep us, O Lord,
in the joy,
the simplicity,
and the compassionate love
of the gospel:
Bless us this day,
and those whom you have given to our care,
through Jesus Christ our Lord.

Together: The grace of our Lord Jesus Christ,
and the love of God,
and the fellowship of the Holy Spirit,
be with us all evermore. Amen.

Intercessions

INTERCESSIONS
1. The Local Church

We offer to God the life of this Christian community:
We pray
That our worship may be marked
by joy and thankfulness,
by peace and true devotion.

That we may live in the spirit of the gospel,
as those who know and love each other;
that we may love and accept the weak and the difficult;
that we may welcome the stranger;
that we may grow together
in love, joy, peace,
patience, kindness, goodness,
faithfulness, humility and discipline.

That we may not despise old things
nor fear the new;
that we may not be discouraged in failure
nor proud in success

That we may witness to our faith
with courage and humility,
with the love and with the patience of Christ:
that we may learn to love people
for their own sake,
and as they are.

For our fellow Christians in this area:
that we may grow in unity
through prayer, through work, through fellowship
and through our witness to the faith we share.

For the leaders of our church, ordained and lay.
May Christ give them his strength,
his love and sensitivity,
his self-forgetfulness
and his faith in the power and wisdom of the Father

For all those who are not members of the Christian Church.
We thank God for them;
for all that we can receive and learn from them.
We give thanks for the love of God
which enfolds us all
in our common humanity.
We pray that in his time they may come to know
the love of God for them.

INTERCESSIONS
2. The Local Community

We thank God for this neighbourhood.
We pray
For good fellowship in our community
and mutual care;
for sensitivity to the needs of others
and the will to act for the common good.
for the reconciliation of those divided;
for the creation of new relationships.

For all our neighbours in this community,
those known to us and unknown,
for families long established
and for newcomers;
that together we may live in harmony,
each seeking the good of others.

For the children and young people,
that they may grow up
with hope in the future.

For the elderly,
that they may enjoy respect,
fulfilment, and freedom from fear.

We thank God for those who minister to human need;
We pray
For all in the caring and teaching professions,
and for those who care at home
for the sick, the handicapped and housebound.

We thank God for our shops and businesses,
our farms and market gardens.
We pray
that they may both prosper and serve the community,
caring beyond their own interests
for the people in this area,
and for the environment,
human, natural and animal.

We thank God for the leaders of our community.
We pray
For those who lead clubs and organisations,
in our community;
for those in local government
that, conscious of the trust placed in them,
they may exercise power with responsibility,
ministering justice and compassion
to all the people in their care.

INTERCESSIONS
3. Suffering

We pray
For all who suffer in mind or body;
for those who are hungry;
for those who suffer from natural disaster
and disease.

For those who suffer oppression
for their beliefs
or their colour.

For the mentally sick
and the physically handicapped;
for all who suffer in their bodies.

For the lonely
and the old;
for those who are suffering bereavement;
for children who suffer.

For those who are anxious or bewildered;
for those who suffer addictions;
for those in prison,
justly or unjustly;
for all who undergo dangers
by land, sea or air.

For all who minister to suffering
that they may be given the grace
of perseverance
and hope.

INTERCESSIONS
4. Peace and Unity

We pray for the peace of the world

For the leaders of the nations,
that a true desire for peace
may overcome jealousy, fear and selfish ambition.
For the United Nations Organisation
and for all who work for reconciliation.

For the nations that are in conflict,
in active warfare
or political enmity;
for nations divided by internal conflict;
for our fellow countrymen
in Northern Ireland.

We pray for the peace of the Church,
for unity and reconciliation among Christians.

We confess our sins against unity:
our lack of humility,
our unreasoning prejudice,
our content with disunity,
our lack of love;
our responsibility through disunity
for hindering the work of Christ
and earning contempt for his name.

We give thanks
for the awakening of the Church
to the need for unity;
and for the signs of unity that exist
throughout the world.

We pray
that in truth and love and hope
we may be brought to that unity
which Christ wills for his Church;
that in a divided world
we may be empowered
to minister the peace of Christ.

INTERCESSIONS
5. Penitence

O Lord, open our minds to see ourselves as you see us,
and from all unwillingness to know our weakness and our sin,
Good Lord, deliver us.

From selfishness;
from wishing to be the centre of attraction;
from seeking admiration;
from the desire to have our own way in all things;
from unwillingness to listen to others;
from resentment of criticism,
Good Lord, deliver us.

From love of power; from jealousy;
from taking pleasure in the weakness of others,
Good Lord, deliver us.

From the weakness of indecision; from fear of adventure;
from constant fear of what others are thinking of us;
from fear of speaking what we know is truth,
and doing what we know is right,
Good Lord, deliver us.

From possessiveness about material things and people;
from carelessness about the needs of others;
from selfish use of time and money;
from all lack of generosity,
Good Lord, deliver us.

From laziness of conscience;
from lack of self-discipline; from failure to persevere;
from depression in failure and disappointment,
Good Lord, deliver us.

From failure to be truthful;
from pretence and acting a part; from hypocrisy;
from all dishonesty with ourselves and with others,
Good Lord, deliver us.

From impurity in word, in thought, and in action;
from failure to respect the bodies and minds
of ourselves and others:
from any kind of addiction,
Good Lord, deliver us.

From hatred and anger; from sarcasm;
from lack of sensitivity to the feelings of others;
from strife and division in our community;
from all failure to love and to forgive,
Good Lord, deliver us.

From failure to see our sin as an affront to God;
from failure to accept the forgiveness he offers,
Good Lord, deliver us.

INTERCESSIONS
6. Holy Communion

In this Holy Sacrifice,
may we be redeemed
by the precious Body and Blood
of our Saviour Jesus Christ:
may our lives be made new in him.

In this Holy Eucharist,
in humble thanksgiving
for the life, suffering and resurrection
of our Lord,
may we offer to him
ourselves, our souls and bodies.

In this Holy Communion,
may we be one in the mystical Body of Christ,
united in loving fellowship
with our Lord,
his saints in heaven,
and our fellow Christians everywhere.

In this Holy Communion,
may we be one with all humanity;
may we offer the joy and sorrow,
the good and evil
of all creation.

In this Holy Memorial of the Last Supper,
may we remember with penitence and joy
his great love for us sinners;
may we offer to him our sacrifice
of praise and thanksgiving.

In this Holy Mystery,
may we abide in him
and he in us.

Calendar of Psalms

JANUARY & JULY DAY		FEBRUARY & AUGUST	MARCH & SEPTEMBER	APRIL & OCTOBER	MAY & NOVEMBER	JUNE & DECEMBER
1	1	30	54(*5)	83(*17)	109(*5-19)	121
2	2	31(1-8)	55(*16-17)	84	110	122
3	3	31(9-27)	56	85	111	123
4	4	32	57	86	112	124
5	5	33(1-12)	59(*6,14)	87	113	125
6	6	33(13-21)	60	88	114	126
7	7	34(1-10)	61	89(1-18)	115	127
8	8	34(11-22)	62	89(19-38)	116	128
9	9	35(1-10)	63	90	117	129
10	10	35(11-29)	64	91	118	130
11	11	36	65	92	119(1-16)	131
12	12	37(1-20)	66	93	119(17-24)	132
13	13	37(21-41)	67	94	119(25-32)	133
14	14	38(1-9)	68(1-20)	95	119(33-40)	134
15	15	38(10-21)	68(24-35)	96	119(41-48)	135
16	16	39	69(*24-30)	97	119(49-56)	136
17	17(*14)	40	70	98	119(57-64)	137(1-6)
18	18(1-31)	41	71(1-14)	99	119(65-72)	138
19	18(32-52)	42	71(15-24)	100	119(73-80)	139(*19-22)
20	19	43	72	101	119(81-88)	140(*9-11)
21	20	44(1-8)	73	102	119(89-96)	141
22	21	44(9-27)	74	103	119(97-104)	142
23	22(1-22)	45	75	104(1-25)	119(105-112)	143(1-11)
24	22(23-32)	46	76	104(26-37)	119(113-120)	144
25	23	47	77	105(1-22)	119(121-128)	145(1-7)
26	24	48	78(1-38)	105(23-45)	119(129-136)	145(8-21)
27	25	49	78(39-70)	106(1-24)	119(137-144)	146
28	26	50(1-15)	79(*10,12)	106(25-50)	119(145-152)	147
29	27	51	80	107(1-22)	119(153-160)	148
30	28	52	81	107(23-43)	119(161-176)	149
31	29	53	82	108	120	150

(*omit these verses)

Calendar of Bible Readings

	JANUARY YEAR 1 *(odd number years)*	JANUARY YEAR 2 *(even number years)*	FEBRUARY	MARCH
1	GENESIS 1.1-19	EXODUS 1	LUKE 1.5-25	ACTS 1.1-14
2	GENESIS 1.20-2:3	EXODUS 2	LUKE 1.26-38	ACTS 2.1-13
3	GENESIS 2.4-25	EXODUS 3	LUKE 1.39-56	ACTS 2.14-36
4	GENESIS 3.1-15	EXODUS 4.1-17	LUKE 1.57-80	ACTS 2.37-47
5	GENESIS 3.16-24	EXODUS 4.18-31	MATT 1.18-25	ACTS 4.1-12
6	GENESIS 4.1-16	EXODUS 5	MATT 2.1-12	ACTS 4.13-31
7	GENESIS 6.9-22	EXODUS 6.1-13	LUKE 2.21-40	ACTS 6.1-7
8	GENESIS 7	EXODUS 6.28—7.13	LUKE 2.41-52	ACTS 6.8-15
9	GENESIS 8	EXODUS 7.14-24	LUKE 3.1-20	ACTS 7.54—8.3
10	GENESIS 9.1-17	EXODUS 11	MATT 3.13—4.11	ACTS 8.14-25
11	GENESIS 11.1-9	EXODUS 12.1-27	LUKE 4.14-30	ACTS 8.26-40
12	GENESIS 12.1-13:1	EXODUS 12.28-51	JOHN 1.35-41	ACTS 9.1-9
13	GENESIS 13.2-18	EXODUS 14.5-20	MARK 1.21-34	ACTS 9.10-25
14	GENESIS 15.1-6	EXODUS 14.21-31	MARK 1.35-45	ACTS 9.32-43
15	GENESIS 17.1-14	EXODUS 16.1-21	MATT 5.1-12	ACTS 10.1-16
16	GENESIS 21.1-12	EXODUS 16.22-36	MATT 5.13-20	ACTS 10.17-29
17	GENESIS 22.1-19	EXODUS 17	MATT 5.21-32	ACTS 10.30-43
18	GENESIS 24.1-27	EXODUS 18	MATT 5.33-48	ACTS 15.1-21
19	GENESIS 24.28-67	EXODUS 19	MATT 6.1-18	ACTS 16.16-40
20	GENESIS 25.19-34	EXODUS 20	MATT 6.19-34	ACTS 17.1-15
21	GENESIS 27.1-29	EXODUS 32.1-14	MATT 7.1-12	ACTS 17.16-34
22	GENESIS 27.30-46	EXODUS 32.15-29	MATT 7.13-29	ACTS 18.1-23
23	GENESIS 28.10-22	DEUT 4.1-13	LUKE 7.1-10	ACTS 18.24—19.7
24	GENESIS 29.1-30	DEUT 5.1-21	MARK 2.1-12	ACTS 19.23-41
25	GENESIS 32.1-23	DEUT 7.6-11	MARK 2.13-17	ACTS 21.1-17
26	GENESIS 32.24—33.11	DEUT 8.1-20	MARK 2.18—3.6	ACTS 21.18-26
27	GENESIS 37.1-24	DEUT 10.11-22	LUKE 10.1-12	ACTS 22.22—23.11
28	GENESIS 37.25-36	DEUT 12.1-11	MATT 10.16-23	ACTS 27.1-26
29	GENESIS 41.1-13	DEUT 26.1-11	MATT 10.24-33	ACTS 27.27-44
30	GENESIS 41.14-45	DEUT 28.1-14		ACTS 28.1-15
31	GENESIS 50.15-26	DEUT 30		ACTS 28.16-31

CALENDAR OF BIBLE READINGS

	APRIL YEAR 1 *(odd number years)*	APRIL YEAR 2 *(even number years)*	MAY	JUNE
1	JOSHUA 1.1-11	2 SAM 1	LUKE 7.36-50	ROMANS 1.1-17
2	JOSHUA 2	2 SAM 7	MARK 3.20-35	ROMANS 2.17-29
3	JOSHUA 5.13—6.11	2 SAM 9	MARK 4.1-12	ROMANS 3.21-31
4	JOSHUA 6.12-23	2 SAM 11	MARK 4.21-34	ROMANS 4.1-12
5	JOSHUA 24.1-25	2 SAM 12.1-25	MARK 5.1-20	ROMANS 5.1-11
6	JUDGES 5.1-18	2 SAM 15.1-15	MARK 5.21-43	ROMANS 6.1-14
7	JUDGES 5.19-31	2 SAM 15.16-37	JOHN 6.1-15	ROMANS 8.1-11
8	JUDGES 7.1-23	2 SAM 16.1-14	MARK 7.1-23	ROMANS 8.12-17
9	JUDGES 13	2 SAM 17.1-23	MARK 7.24-37	ROMANS 8.18-30
10	JUDGES 14	2 SAM 18.1-18	MATT 16.13-23	ROMANS 8.1-39
11	JUDGES 15	2 SAM 18.19-33	MATT 16.24-28	ROMANS 12.1-8
12	JUDGES 16	2 SAM 24	LUKE 9.28-36	ROMANS 12.9-21
13	RUTH 1	1 KINGS 1.5-31	MARK 9.14-29	ROMANS 13.7-14
14	RUTH 2	1 KINGS 1.38-53	MARK 9.30-37	ROMANS 14.19—15.6
15	RUTH 3	1 KINGS 2.1-12	MATT 18.23-25	ROMANS 15.14-21
16	RUTH 4.1-17	1 KINGS 3.3-15	LUKE 10.25-37	ROMANS 15.22-33
17	1 SAM 1.1-20	1 KINGS 8.1-21	LUKE 10.38-42	1 COR 1.1-9
18	1 SAM 3.1-19	1 KINGS 11.26-40	LUKE 11.1-13	1 COR 1.10-17
19	1 SAM 9.1-14	1 KINGS 11.43—12.16	LUKE 11.37-54	1 COR 1.18-31
20	1 SAM 9.15—10.1	1 KINGS 17.1-16	LUKE 13.10-17	1 COR 2
21	1 SAM 15.1-23	1 KINGS 18.1-29	LUKE 14.7-14	1 COR 3.1-17
22	1 SAM 16	1 KINGS 18.30-46	LUKE 14.15-24	1 COR 3.18-23
23	1 SAM 17.1-25	1 KINGS 19	LUKE 15.11-32	1 COR 12.1-11
24	1 SAM 17.26-50	1 KINGS 21.1-16	LUKE 16.19-31	1 COR 12.12-31
25	1 SAM 18.1-16	1 KINGS 21.17-29	LUKE 17.11-19	1 COR 13
26	1 SAM 19.1-18	2 KINGS 2.1-15	LUKE 18.9-14	1 COR 14.26-40
27	1 SAM 20.1-23	2 KINGS 4.1-17	MARK 10.1-12	1 COR 15.1-9
28	1 SAM 20.24-42	2 KINGS 5	MARK 10.15-16	1 COR 15.20-34
29	1 SAM 24	2 KINGS 24.8-17	MARK 10.17-27	1 COR 15.35-49
30	1 SAM 31	2 KINGS 24.18—25.12	MATT 20.1-16	1 COR 15.50-58
31			MATT 20.20-28	

CALENDAR OF BIBLE READINGS

	JULY YEAR 1 *(odd number years)*	JULY YEAR 2 *(even number years)*	AUGUST	SEPTEMBER
1	AMOS 2	EZEK 2:3—3.11	LUKE 19:1-10	2 COR 1.1-14
2	AMOS 3.1-8	EZEK 3:12-27	LUKE 19:11-27	2 COR 2.5-17
3	AMOS 6.1-8	EZEK 8.1-12	MARK 11.1-10	2 COR 3.1-6
4	AMOS 8.1-12	EZEK 11.14-25	MATT 21.10-17	2 COR 4.1-15
5	AMOS 9.8-15	EZEK 12.1-16	MARK 12.1-12	2 COR 4.16—5.10
6	HOSEA 1.1—2:1	EZEK 14.12-23	MARK 12.28-34	2 COR 5.11—6.2
7	HOSEA 2.14—3.5	EZEK 18	MATT 25.31-46	2 COR 12.1-10
8	HOSEA 6.1-6	EZEK 24.15-27	MARK 14.1-11	GAL 1.1-10
9	HOSEA 11.1-9	EZEK 33.1-20	MARK 14.12-31	GAL 2.11-21
10	HOSEA 14	EZEK 33.21-33	MARK 14.32-52	GAL 3.1-6
11	ISAIAH 1.1-20	EZEK 34.1-16	LUKE 22.54-71	GAL 3.7-22
12	ISAIAH 5.1-23	EZEK 34.17-31	JOHN 18.28-40	GAL 5.13-25
13	ISAIAH 6.1-12	EZEK 36.16-38	JOHN 19.1-16	EPHES 1.1-14
14	ISAIAH 7.10-17	EZEK 37.1-14	MATT 27.27-50	EPHES 1.15-23
15	ISAIAH 11.10-16	EZEK 39.21-29	LUKE 23.26-38	EPHES 2.1-10
16	ISAIAH 12	ISAIAH 40.1-11	LUKE 23.39-49	EPHES 2.11-22
17	ISAIAH 26.1-10	ISAIAH 40.25-31	JOHN 19.17-37	EPHES 3.1-13
18	JEREMIAH 1.1-19	ISAIAH 41.8-20	JOHN 19.38-42	EPHES 3.14-21
19	JEREMIAH 2.4-13	ISAIAH 42.1-9	MARK 15.40-47	PHIL 1.27—2.13
20	JEREMIAH 5.1-9	ISAIAH 42.10-25	MATT 27.55-66	PHIL 3.1-16
21	JEREMIAH 8.18—9.3	ISAIAH 43.1-15	MARK 16.1-8	COL 1.1-20
22	JEREMIAH 15.10-21	ISAIAH 43.16-28	MATT 28.1-10	COL 1.21—2.5
23	JEREMIAH 18.1-23	ISAIAH 44.1-22	MATT 28.16-20	COL 2.6—3.4
24	JEREMIAH 21.1-10	ISAIAH 44.23-28	JOHN 20.1-9	COL 3.5-17
25	JEREMIAH 22.13-30	ISAIAH 45.18-25	JOHN 20.10-18	1 THESS 2.1-12
26	JEREMIAH 23.16-29	ISAIAH 49.1-13	JOHN 20.19-31	1 THESS 4.13-18
27	JEREMIAH 26	ISAIAH 50	JOHN 21.1-14	1 THESS 5.1-11
28	JEREMIAH 29.1-14	ISAIAH 51.1-11	JOHN 21.15-25	1 THESS 5.12-28
29	JEREMIAH 31.23-40	ISAIAH 52.13—53.6	LUKE 24.1-11	2 THESS 2.1-12
30	JEREMIAH 38.1-13	ISAIAH 53.7-12	LUKE 24.13-32	2 THESS 2.13-17
31	JEREMIAH 39	ISAIAH 56.1-8	LUKE 24.33-53	

CALENDAR OF BIBLE READINGS

	OCTOBER YEAR 1 *(odd number years)*	OCTOBER YEAR 2 *(even number years)*	NOVEMBER	DECEMBER
1	DANIEL 1	JOB 1	JOHN 1.1-14	HEBREWS 1
2	DANIEL 2.1-23	JOB 2	JOHN 2.1-11	HEBREWS 2.10-18
3	DANIEL 2.24-46	JOB 3.1-19	JOHN 3.1-12	HEBREWS 3.1-11
4	DANIEL 3.1-18	JOB 4.1-17	JOHN 3.13-21	HEBREWS 5.11—6.12
5	DANIEL 3.19-30	JOB 6.1-13	JOHN 3.22-36	HEBREWS 6.13-20
6	DANIEL 4.1-18	JOB 13.1-15	JOHN 4.1-26	HEBREWS 7.15-28
7	DANIEL 4.19-37	JOB 14.1-14	JOHN 5.1-15	HEBREWS 9.1-14
8	DANIEL 5.1-12	JOB 19.13-27	JOHN 5.24-30	HEBREWS 11.1-16
9	DANIEL 5.13-30	JOB 28.1-11	JOHN 5.31-47	HEBREWS 12.1-17
10	DANIEL 6.1-14	JOB 28.12-28	JOHN 6.22-29	HEBREWS 13.1-16
11	DANIEL 6.15-28	JOB 38.1-21	JOHN 6.30-45	JAMES 1.1-11
12	DANIEL 9.1-19	JOB 38.22-41	JOHN 6.46-58	JAMES 1.22-27
13	DANIEL 10.1-14	JOB 39	JOHN 7.37-52	JAMES 2.1-13
14	DANIEL 12	JOB 40	JOHN 8.12-20	JAMES 2.14-26
15	EZRA 1	JOB 42	JOHN 9.13-38	1 PETER 1.1-12
16	EZRA 3	PROVERBS 1.20-23	JOHN 10.1-18	1 PETER 1.13-25
17	EZRA 7.11-28	PROVERBS 3.11-20	JOHN 11.1-16	1 PETER 2.1-10
18	NEHEMIAH 1	PROVERBS 4	JOHN 11.17-44	1 PETER 2.11-25
19	NEHEMIAH 2	PROVERBS 6.6-19	JOHN 11.45-57	1 PETER 3.1-12
20	NEHEMIAH 4.1-23	PROVERBS 8.1-21	JOHN 12.20-36	1 JOHN 1.1—2.5
21	NEHEMIAH 6.1-15	PROVERBS 8.22-36	JOHN 13.1-17	1 JOHN 2.6-17
22	NEHEMIAH 8.1-18	PROVERBS 9.1-10	JOHN 14.1-14	1 JOHN 2.18-29
23	NEHEMIAH 13.15-22	PROVERBS 10.1-13	JOHN 14.15-21	1 JOHN 4
24	JONAH 1.1-16	PROVERBS 12.9-22	JOHN 14.22-31	REVEL'N 1
25	JONAH 1.17—2.10	PROVERBS 14.1-12	JOHN 15.1-10	
26	JONAH 3	PROVERBS 14.27-35	JOHN 15.11-17	REVEL'N 3.7-22
27	JONAH 4	PROVERBS 15.1-15	JOHN 15.18-27	REVEL'N 4
28	ZECHARIAH 1.7-21	PROVERBS 15.16-33	JOHN 16.12-24	REVEL'N 5
29	ZECHARIAH 2	PROVERBS 30.1-9	JOHN 16.25-33	REVEL'N 21.1-7
30	ZECHARIAH 8.1-13	PROVERBS 30.15-31	JOHN 17	REVEL'N 21.15-27
31	ZECHARIAH 8.14-23	PROVERBS 31.10-31		REVEL'N 22

APPENDIX

'A New Pattern for Sunday Worship'
(The text of an address by the author in Norwich Cathedral 21 July 1991)

When the Archbishop of Canterbury addressed the Readers in Birmingham last month he said, '. . . In my last diocese I dreamed of a development contemplated in the strategy of the Bishop of Norwich for his own diocese – the goal of a service . . . in every town or village at, say, ten o'clock every Sunday morning . . .'

That extract was reported in a national newspaper, and caused me some surprise, because Archbishops are not always noted for acknowledging the sources of their ideas. The report has been followed by a good deal of correspondence, not to say controversy. It has been said, for instance, that this would put even more strain on rural clergy who are already overworked, and that it is impractical to have a service at the same time in every church. Now both of these criticisms are based on a misunderstanding about what precisely the Archbishop was intending, and so it might perhaps be helpful if I set out what my original proposals actually were.

It all started some years ago when I was a suffragan in Somerset. I was visiting a group of rural parishes with five churches, small congregations and a population of just under 1000. I was invited to talk to a joint meeting of the Church Councils about the future. I think they expected me to grasp the nettle and suggest that one or more of their churches should close.

The evening began with a description of the pattern of services in the churches. It was the usual combination of 1st, 3rd and 5th Sundays here at 10.30 am, 2nd Sunday there at 11.15 am, 4th Sunday elsewhere at 8 am and 6.30 pm, and so forth. You cannot worship in the countryside these days unless you are armed with a duplicated sheet of paper giving the incredibly complex computations of times, dates and places of worship. This might be all right for the very committed, but would-be occasional worshippers and holidaymakers, both of which are significant groups, are understandably daunted by the complexity and tend not to bother.

Anyway, after examining the pattern of services there was a pause while they braced themselves for the onslaught of the episcopal axe. Instead I said: 'I think you should be having far more services in all your churches: in fact you should have a service at the same time every Sunday in every church'. The assembled colonels, farmers and their wives, retired bank managers and secretaries of WIs raised their heads from the executioner's block and stared in disbelief. Then I launched for the first time into my vision for the future of rural worship, which at that time was only half-formed. But really it is very simple.

As clergy numbers have fallen, so worship in the countryside has been reduced to fit the capacity of priests and available readers to circulate round the churches. Some say this has been a sensible cutting of the coat according to the cloth. Actually I think it is much more sinister. What is happening is that rural worship is dying the death of a thousand cuts.

Part of the difficulty has been caused paradoxically by the very success of the Parish Communion movement in establishing the Holy Communion as the central act of worship in churches of all traditions. Village congregations, like their urban counterparts, have been well taught in this regard and many now expect eucharistic worship to be the norm. This is part of the reason for the frantic Sunday rush around the parishes that is the stressful lot of far too many rural clergy. I believe that the centrality of the Holy Communion is theologically right. It is quite clearly a truth of scripture and tradition, and its renewal in the Church of England has been a great blessing. But there has been associated with it a devaluing of worship which is not eucharistic. Furthermore a certain equation has been assumed which I believe needs to be questioned. Eucharistic centrality has been equated with regular communion. That is obviously right, but a further equation has been made, that regular communion equals frequent communion. The ideal has therefore become communion every week in every church. That is an ideal which is practicable in most urban parishes, but it is not feasible in the country without intolerable strain being put upon the ordained ministry. For people of my age, including those who were brought up in a catholic tradition, regular communion meant receiving the sacrament monthly, not weekly. I do not think one suffered spiritually through that discipline, which is just one reason why I think our modern assumptions need to be re-examined. Regular communion need not mean, everywhere and for everyone, frequent communion. It certainly cannot mean that in Africa and many parts of Asia.

From these reflections comes what I know some may regard as an unrealistic hope, but which I believe more and more is something that can be done, which ought to be done, and if done would prove to be of incalculable significance for the mission of the Church.

I believe that there should be a corporate act of worship in every community, however tiny, on every Sunday. In worship Christians offer themselves to God in penitence, praise and thanksgiving. They reflect on God's word and intercede for those in need. When Christians worship in their church it is a community activity in two senses. First, it is the church in that place, the Christian community at prayer, and joining in the prayer of the whole Church in heaven and on earth. Secondly, that Christian group is at prayer on behalf of the community of the village or town or neighbourhood in which they live, representing those who do not, cannot, or will not worship themselves. The Christian life follows the pattern of Christ's life lived for others, and that living for others begins with prayer for others. It is the corporate worship of the Church Sunday by Sunday in which that prayer for the whole community is focussed.

It would be a wonderful thing if we could advertise in every village, however tiny, and every neighbourhood, that God is worshipped here at such and such a time. Not, I hasten to add, that worship should take place in every single church building necessarily, but in every single community, and if it is at all possible, that service should take place at the same time each Sunday. I do not mean – and here the remarks of the Archbishop have been misunderstood – that the same time should be chosen for every church. I mean that, for example, a notice would read that 'In this church there will be an act of worship at 9.30 am every Sunday'; in the next village the notice would advertise a service at 11.30 am or some other time. The time for each community would be different, but would ideally be the same time for that particular church each week.

If this is to be attempted, let alone achieved, certain important factors should be borne in mind. First, this is out of the question for clergy. They are stretched beyond their limits, most of them, already. It is out of the question to have lay Readers being responsible. In this diocese, like some others, there are more Readers than clergy, but even so there are simply not enough of them. These acts of worship, these weekly times of prayer, would have to be led by ordinary lay men and women from the congregations. In order to do that there would need some simple form of training; not much, because we would not expect them of course to preach a sermon. It is the common experience of bishops, as they travel up and down their dioceses week by week, that on most Sundays we are part of an act of worship in which lay people participate as lesson readers and leaders of intercession. Very often they convey a remarkable natural instinct for leading worship. There are hundreds of such people in every diocese who could easily lead a simple act of worship every week, given a simple form of training.

The second consideration is that we should not worry about numbers. In a tiny community maybe only half-a-dozen would muster to pray together each week, maybe two or three, maybe only one. But even if a single Christian prays alone, but publicly in church, through him or her the whole church is at worship and the whole community is represented and presented to God in loving intercession.

It is common in country areas for small parishes to group together to worship from time to time, usually once a quarter on the fifth Sunday, sometimes once a month or so. My proposal might seem to undermine that group worship and fellowship, and indeed be a surrender to those who obstinately refuse to worship anywhere except in their own parish church. That would not be the intention, for the joining of worship on a grander scale than is possible in a single small community is right and good and has in many rural areas transformed people's experience of worship. But I do not believe that unity in a group of parishes is achieved by over-emphasis on united worship, and can be counter productive if it is perceived as a reduction in worship in individual communities. Moreover, we should remember that the grouping of parishes is largely artificial, a method of organising the Church's life, and does not thereby create new communities on a larger scale. Regular united acts of worship in which a number of congregations join is to be encouraged, but I do not believe that this is incompatible with weekly worship in the individual congregation. I believe one should also have the humility to acknowledge the possibility that God may be speaking to us through the apparently obstinate parishioner who refuses to join in these things, because underneath what may be interpreted as narrow-mindedness, may be an unconscious witness to a principle that on the Lord's Day each community, however small, should be at prayer.

In an era of increasing centralisation it is necessary to emphasise the importance of locality, to affirm the local community, however small, however insignificant it feels itself to be. It need not, and understood rightly, does not, detract from the sense of participation in the wider community.

My expectation is that sometimes a priest would come and there would be a celebration of Holy Communion; sometimes a Reader, and a sermon would be preached. But the continuity, the regular worshipping life of the church in that place, would depend not on a Priest or a Reader, but on local people who pray and lead their neighbours in prayer faithfully week by week.

It is important finally to accept that this worship on a small scale might not always feel uplifting. Often music will not be possible or wise; no sermons to criticise or praise; no feeding through the sacrament. The trouble is that in the Church of England congregations in some places tend to regard worship rather in the manner of an audience. By that I mean we tend to judge an act of worship by whether it was well done or badly done; by the quality and length of the sermon; and the music. In short, by our reaction to it and whether we got something out of it or not. But that is not the purpose of worship. It is quite simply to give worth to God. It is God we try to please in worship, not ourselves. Whether we 'get something out of it' or not is strictly irrelevant. We do it for God, because we love him, and our love for him, like all true love, must often be expressed as duty. The old monks used to call their daily prayer the Opus Dei, 'the work of God'. It was their first responsibility and they did it for him, whether they felt like it or not; it was their duty and it was a way of loving him. So I hope the church will take seriously the possibility of an Opus Dei in every rural parish as a way of persevering love for God and care for our neighbours.

Its effects are literally not calculable, but I believe would be transforming. It has particular relevance to the Decade of Evangelism, because unless our mission is girded with prayer the seed will fall on stony ground. The purpose of worship is not evangelism. Its purpose is to express our love for God. But there is no doubt that through worship men and women, young and old, can be, and are, drawn into commitment to Christ.